30 Minutes
... To Master
the Internet

GW00342493

30 Minutes
... To Master
the Internet

Steven Armstrong

**Fully updated
2nd edition**

KOGAN
PAGE

To Ben and Chaz for being the greatest

First published in 1997
Author: Neil Barrett

Second edition published in 2001
Author: Steven Armstrong

Kogan Page Limited
120 Pentonville Road
London N1 9JN
UK

British Library Cataloguing in Publication Data
A CIP record for this book is available from the British Library.

ISBN 0 7494 3502 X

Typeset by Saxon Graphics Ltd, Derby

Printed and bound in Great Britain by Clays Ltd, St Ives plc

CONTENTS

INTRODUCTION

If you need to manage the Internet at work but don't have the time to learn about it, this book is for you. It is not the usual Internet guide designed to tell you how to use the Internet at home. This book is designed for anyone who needs to quickly understand the Internet, its challenges, how it works and its potential rewards in the workplace.

The book is therefore designed as a series of 5-minute briefings, and in total should take only 30 minutes to read. Our challenge has been to distil the information into short, punchy text that still delivers all of the latest technology along with how to use it and what considerations you should take into account, either as an employee or as an employer.

Because home working is as common as office working we cover working from home as well as working from the office and working on the move.

We cover everything from technology choices to strategies for effective use, saving money and formulating policy to cover the legal and other implications of working in a 'connected' environment. Throughout the book you will also find 'tips' – these are useful snippets of information of the type that you usually only find out through hard-won experience. You will also find:

JARGON BUSTERS

Throughout the book you will find jargon busters, short descriptions that allow you to understand the issues normally hidden by 'techno speak'.

Our Web site is here to help you further

Normally in an executive briefing you would be able to ask questions to confirm your understanding or to follow up on a particular area of interest. We have therefore developed a Web site to accompany the book where you can find links to many useful technologies and suppliers who are mentioned generically in the book.

1

GETTING STARTED

Getting started on the Internet may look like an expensive and daunting business, but it need not be. In fact, getting online is relatively simple and straightforward, and need not require a great deal of time and effort. With a little forethought and planning the Internet can become an invaluable tool for both you and your organization and can even save you money.

If you are a new user to the Internet you will need three things to get online:

- a connection to the Internet;
- a computer system;
- an Internet Service Provider.

Connecting to the Internet

For most of us, this means the basic connection made up of two elements: a modem and a standard telephone line.

In this basic scenario, information flows along the telephone line that connects you to the Internet in the form of 'bits' of information. Bits are basically 1s and 0s. These two digits are used to encode a word or any other piece of data that needs to be passed along the telephone line. Therefore, a word such as 'and' may be represented as 01101000111101110 in its digital form. The speed with which the telephone line can transmit these coded 'bits' is measured in 'bits per second', often written as 'bps'. For example, you may come across:

- 9,600 bps (slow).
- 14.4 Kbps. In this case the 'K' means 1000, so 14.4 Kbps may also be written as 14,400 bps, which is obviously better than 9,600 bps but is still slow.
- 28.8 Kbps.
- 56 Kbps.

Occasionally Kbps may just be referred to as 'K' and so 56 Kbps may become just 56 K.

So we now have a measure of the speed at which information can be passed by the telephone line from the Internet to your modem. Your modem is the piece of technology that receives these signals from the telephone line and passes them to your computer. The speed with which your modem does this is also measured in bits per second, or bps.

Therefore, we can see that the best combination of line speed and modem speed is one where the two components are matched as having a 56 K line and having only a 14.4 K modem, or a 56 K modem and only a 14.4 K line, will mean that information will only be passed to your computer at the lowest common denominator of 14.4 Kbps.

When choosing your computer, therefore, the speed at which the modem can operate is a crucial factor to consider. When choosing your Internet connection the line speed is a crucial factor to consider.

In this type of arrangement, where each computer is connected to the Internet individually, each computer is said to be 'stand-alone', as opposed to the scenario where a number of computers are joined to an internal network before that network is connected to the Internet.

The office network

In many office environments your computer may already be connected to an internal network. This may also be called a LAN (Local Area Network). When you start your computer you will usually be asked for a password to sign on to the network (meaning the internal network rather than the Internet). After 'signing on' you usually have access to the Internet as well as to shared resources such as printers, internal mail services, file sharing, etc.

In this environment the Internet is usually 'always present' or 'always on' and when you open your Internet browser you are immediately connected to the Internet. This is usually because the local area network that you are connected to has a permanent connection to the Internet. Your computer in this scenario does not have a modem connecting it to the internal network but rather a 'network adaptor' or 'network card', sometimes called an 'Ethernet card'. These network adaptors or cards are capable of handling much higher rates of transmission than a modem and so you should experience good performance from your Internet connection with pages loading quickly.

JARGON BUSTER

The speed of a telecoms connection to the Internet and the speed of an internal network are both sometimes referred to as 'bandwidth', meaning the amount of data that can be squeezed down the same line at the same time. The higher the bandwidth, the more data that can be transmitted along it. Rather like water in a pipe, the wider the pipe, the more water that can flow along it.

What is a firewall?

Very often, in-between the office network and the open connection to the outside world and all that is available on the Internet is a safety device called a firewall. This is, in fact, a computer and may sometimes be referred to in an office environment as the 'Internet server'. The firewall server will be connected on one side to the Internet and on the other to the internal network. The job of the firewall is to act as a protective shield so that any viruses or hackers with intent to disrupt the company's main computers are stopped before they gain access to the company's internal network. These machines are therefore usually 'loaded to the teeth' with software designed to detect any hostile intent coming from outside, be it a virus or a hacker. The danger is that once either a virus or a hacker gain access to the company's internal network they can go anywhere on that network and so they can access any or even all of the machines connected to that network. In practice this means that you may be limited, depending on the level of security, in what you may access on 'The Outside' or you may not be able to dial in from home unless you use a specific machine or specific passwords. All of this is necessary, as one can imagine the financial and other impact of illegal access to companies' internal systems. Later in this book we will look in more detail at the issues surrounding security when using the Internet or establishing an online presence.

JARGON BUSTER

Hackers are now more commonly known as 'black hats' and they even have their own annual convention. Some claim to only 'hack' sites such as pornography sites with the intention of rendering them unusable. These 'good' hackers refer to themselves as 'grey hats'.

Higher speed connections

If office systems are usually connected together via an Internal LAN or network, what do these internal networks use to connect to the Internet?

The leased line

The leased line is the predominant means of connection for almost all business use. A leased line is a permanent connection to an Internet Service Provider (ISP) and because it is a dedicated and direct link it is always connected, consequently there is no need to 'dial in' to your ISP – they are always there and you are always online. Leased lines are expensive because you are the only user of the line, and because they are expensive they are usually confined to an office of a reasonable size where there are a medium to large number of computers to be connected. In this scenario, the number of computers sharing the leased line makes it an economically sensible proposition, as to connect each computer via a modem and telephone line would a) cost more, b) give each user worse performance and c) cause contention for available lines unless each computer was assigned its own line.

Leased lines, therefore, are generally for an office of medium to large size and are not generally an option for branch offices or for home use.

ISDN

ISDN, or Integrated Services Digital Network, is a digital alternative to the dial-up modem. ISDN is increasingly being offered by the large telecoms companies as an alternative to modem connection. The digital nature means that this connection is many times faster than a standard telephone line connection, both in the speed at which data is transferred down the line and in the speed at which one can connect. Connecting to your ISP over an ISDN line normally takes less than a second. As it costs considerably less than a leased line and is usually quicker to install. ISDN is generally marketed as an alternative to a full leased line service either for smaller businesses or for branch offices or offices at home.

ADSL

ADSL (Asymmetric Digital Subscriber Line) and DSL (Digital Subscriber Line) are the current buzz of the telecommunications industry. Both are new ways of providing high-speed Internet access and bear much resemblance to ISDN. Like ISDN, you need to have a 'terminal adaptor' to link your computer to this type of line, as a modem would prove too slow and not be able to handle the staggering speeds of which ADSL and DSL are capable.

What speed are we talking about? Well, ADSL can provide 32 Mbps from the Internet to your computer – that's

50 times the speed of the basic ISDN line (and over 600 times as fast as a standard telephone line and modem configuration!). The speed going back the other way, ie from your computer to the Internet, is somewhat less, as the technology varies the speed between the top rate of 32 Mbps and a guaranteed minimum of 1 Mbps but this is still an astonishing increase over the standard line and modem.

The other main difference between this type of service and most others available today is that it is really designed for the Internet age. It is permanently connected and is usually charged at a 'flat rate' per month rather than by metered usage. This type of line gives smaller businesses and individuals working from home the 'always on' and high-speed advantages previously only available to businesses who could afford a leased line connection.

Choosing the right computer system

There are many different types of computer that can be connected to the Internet. PDAs and WAP phones can be connected, as well as PCs and Macs. Add to this the fact that the technology is moving at an increasingly fast pace and you may wonder how on earth you are expected to know which system is the right one to go online with.

The thing to remember is that all of these technology choices are just that – choices – they let you, the consumer, choose the system that best reflects your working lifestyle and the uses to which your system will be put. So let's see if we can narrow the criteria into a more manageable set of options.

What style of computer do you need?

First, do you want full access to the Internet or just access to e-mail? If the answer is that you only want to access e-mail and will never want more than that, then there are a host of low-cost e-mail devices to choose from, many at budget prices. If, however, you want to access the wealth of Internet sites as well as sending and receiving e-mail then you have a different choice.

The next decision is: do you want access to the Internet on the move or is a desktop device adequate? If your choice is for a mobile connection to the Internet then you may want to consider a WAP phone or a PDA system rather than a full-blown laptop.

What is a WAP phone?

WAP (Wireless Application Protocol) phones are the latest generation of European and UK mobile telephones. (There is a competitor in Japan called 'imode' but this is not an internationally agreed standard at the present time.) These systems are more than just a conventional mobile telephone as they enable one to access WAP-enabled Web sites and to send and receive e-mail messages straight from the phone. The attraction of WAP is in its mobility and the fact that you need only the telephone; no other equipment is required.

WAP, however, has its limitations; until the next generation of mobile phones arrives the connection speed is slow and the size of the screen on WAP phones is small. Battery technology and screen technology is improving though, and WAP phone screen sizes will get bigger and eventually colour and high resolution will become commonplace. Currently, WAP phones can only access WAP converted or WAP-enabled sites and this means that you may not be able to access the sites you want.

In its favour, though, because of the limitations of the technology, WAP sites tend to be designed for people who simply want a specific piece of information quickly and then to get off the site as fast as possible. This makes them

14

very attractive in areas such as results services, picking up e-mails remotely, share-watch services, etc. WAP-enabled sites can also be set up to automatically call you with an 'alert', ie with the result of an auction, or the opportunity to place a bid if someone else has outbid you, or if your share portfolio has dropped below a certain trigger point, or if you have just received a fax at the office.

WAP then is very good at some things but has a way to go before it becomes as all-encompassing as the conventional Internet.

What is a PDA or palmtop?

A PDA is a Personal Digital Assistant. Psion was the pioneer of the PDA world with its small, highly functional machines that gave you office systems in very small, hand-held devices. Functions such as a diary and an address book combine with e-mail and Internet access to make a highly functional 'office on the move' package. Some PDAs and palmtops also offer word-processing, spreadsheets and other office applications. Some can also provide guides, maps, language converters and many more software applications. Many PDAs also offer slick 'hot synching' to a main computer system or other PDAs.

As well as Psion, 3com, Hewlett Packard, Compaq and many others run either their own custom-built software or Windows CE, a specially engineered version of the Windows operating system.

JARGON BUSTER

To 'hot synch' means to connect two computers and have them update one another automatically when connected. In this way, for example, a PDA can, by hot

---

synching, exchange diary and contact information that has changed with another computer, say with your desktop at home or at work. The two systems will coordinate the changes that have been made on each since they were last connected. In this way new diary or address book additions (or deletions) can be exchanged and a new coordinated version derived. The whole process is usually managed by a piece of software, the two machines being connected either by a specialized linking cable or by two-way infrared communications ports.

If you are looking for a package where the main access to the Internet will be for sending or retrieving e-mail or for limited use of the Internet (ie not for prolonged use or more complex use such as development where a large screen is a necessity) then a PDA may offer everything you need. The choice, though, as to whether a PDA is sufficient on its own or whether a main laptop or desktop is needed tends to rely on the need for other software applications rather than on Internet access.

Laptop and desktop systems

In this category there are two main types to choose from: PC compatibles and Apple Macintosh. As a bit of history, PC compatibles are so named as IBM produced the first ones and therefore anyone else who at that time produced a similar product badged it as 'IBM PC compatible,' gradually the IBM denotation dropped away, mainly because Microsoft became the dominant force rather than IBM. If you choose a PC compatible it will almost certainly come with Windows; if it does not you may want to look at others that provide Windows as part of the package. In the debate over whether to buy a compatible (Windows) PC or an Apple Macintosh there are strong arguments either way, and in general people will either fall into one camp or the other, and once in such a camp usually refuse to switch to the other. Apple has always produced systems that look very stylish and the current range look particularly good. Windows PC manufacturers, however, are waking up to style and there are a few good-looking desktops and laptops around. In the main, your choice should be to get the latest system possible with the most processing power and disk storage for the price. In Internet terms, the only thing that matters is processing speed, as this affects the machine's ability to handle graphics and modem speed. Screen sizes, and so on, are then personal choice items.

TIP

If you are travelling the globe with your laptop and you want to get help and advice about connecting to the Internet from various parts of the world, look up www.laptoptravel.com.
too happy to tell you so.

2

HOW TO USE THE
WORLD WIDE WEB

The World Wide Web is a wonderful tool that, if used efficiently, can bring huge benefits to your organization, and can actually reduce costs. In this chapter we look at how to utilize the Web for your benefit and how to formulate a policy to stop misuse or spiralling costs.

What is the Internet?

The Internet is a number of separate networks that have, over time and as linking technologies matured, become connected. These connected networks are called the Internet. Different people therefore own pieces of the Internet; these pieces are called 'the backbone'. Information flows seamlessly across the backbone regardless of the different owners of the various pieces. Each piece of backbone runs over very high-speed links between two computers that each belong to someone. Each of these computers is therefore a place where someone could link to the Internet. The owners of some of these computers share them with people who want to attach to the Internet. When they do this, they are called Internet Service Providers (ISPs). One side of the ISP's computer is attached to the Net, the other to telephone lines of various speeds to which you attach your computer. You therefore pay for the line rental and usage of the local line to get from your machine to the ISP. The ISP then pays for their stretch of the backbone, which sometimes they buy in bulk or sometimes they even own themselves and here lies the place where you can make very substantial savings for your organization by using the connectivity of the Internet. (More in a moment.)

So that the system knows how to send information from one place to another place when a computer is joined to the Internet, it is given a unique address and there is a system of registries that record in huge databases what all of the addresses are and who is at each one. Because an ISP is in business to rent out millions of slices of their computer resource, their computers are like blocks of apartments with hundreds or thousands of addresses all in the same place.

There, that's it! The Internet then is a vast collection of computers networked together. OK, I hear you say, so if that's the Internet, what is the World Wide Web?

The World Wide Web

The World Wide Web is one of a number of facilities that runs over the Internet and uses a specific 'protocol' to transfer documents called the Hypertext Transfer Protocol (HTTP). Although the Web has become synonymous for many people with the Internet and the two words are often used to mean the same thing, they are not the same as the

Internet allows other protocols such as File Transfer Protocol (FTP) to run across it.

The World Wide Web was invented by a researcher in Switzerland who got tired of searching amongst millions of documents posted all over the Internet to find the one he wanted and thought that there must be a better way of doing it. Tim Berners-Lee then invented a method by which documents or files could point to other documents or files by using a linking device called a hyperlink. He then invented a browser so that he could see the links and jump from one to another. In this way, documents and files formed a sort of a web, like a spider's web with interconnected strands, and as it became very popular it spread worldwide. So the World Wide Web is really just a method of indexing.

The World Wide Web is actually therefore a collection of linked pages and files. A page can contain data in the form of words or pictures. There is a language called HTML which controls how a piece of text or a graphic is displayed on a page, ie what colour(s) it is, does it blink, is it animated, etc. Pages are joined together by hyperlinks and hyperlinks can link pages, which are stored anywhere on the Internet, even on opposite sides of the world. This is done by giving every page its own unique address on the Internet called a URL (a Uniform Resource Locator). A collection of linked pages is called a Web site. A Web browser allows us to view all of these pages without having to download or convert them from one format to another.

Finding your way around the Web

If you've not used the Web before, don't worry – you can't break it, plus there are some very easy to use navigation tools that will help you to get around the system and understand what is happening.

First on your browser you will have, at the top of the screen, a menu bar. This will usually have forward and back buttons either as text or as arrows pointing right (forward) and left (back). You can use these to go back to the last page you were on (and the pages before that) and then forward again until you reach the most current page.

Next there are buttons such as 'home' (you might have a little picture of a house), which will take you from wherever you are now to your home page. (Usually your ISP's home page, unless you have set another page as 'home.') This is so you can always go back to a common starting point from which you know your way to other places. You will also find 'refresh' for when the page you asked for next doesn't seem to be loading or only half appears and then freezes. Refresh just reorders the same page again without you having to type in the page name. One of the most annoying things on the Web is when you find a really great site and then can't remember the address when you want to go back to it at another time. 'Favourites' or 'Bookmarks' allow you to make a note of a page that you want to go back to again and keep it in an address book that you can arrange in a way that suits you.

Underneath this row of icons or buttons there is the address bar. This usually has a white space in which the address of the page you are in appears. This usually takes the following form: www. the site name. country code/the name of the page itself. You can type into the address bar the address of a site that you want to visit (if you know it) and go there directly by either hitting return or clicking the mouse. If you want to try this for yourself to see if you have mastered navigating the World Wide Web, try typing in 'www.StevenArmstrong.com/helppage' and if you get it right there will be a special message waiting there for you to read.

Other useful things to note are that you usually have an empty square in the bottom left of the screen, which shows the progress of the page loading; the bar moves (right) across it as loading progresses, a little like a digital speedometer. Sometimes you will also get a percentage figure in the bottom right of the screen. If neither of these is moving or if the mouse pointer has not changed to the 'working' status (usually an egg timer) then nothing is going on, so try clicking again or clicking refresh. If you clicked when you didn't mean to there is a 'stop' button on the menu bar.

At the top right of your screen there are also the three signs to control screen size. Clicking on the '–' shrinks this screen down to a box at the bottom of the screen. A box or two boxes overlapped makes the screen size either full or half-sized, respectively. Lastly, there is an 'x', which means delete this screen.

These screen controls are important. Some of my friends find using the Web confusing as they don't realize that the Web site that they are using may open up more than one screen and overlay new screens on old ones but leave the old ones open so that you can go back to them by shrinking the current 'uppermost' screen and then using the open ones underneath. I personally think that this is bad design but nevertheless they are out there so I hope this little guide helps. If all else fails, use the back button or go back to your home page and try something that's designed rather better.

Using the World Wide Web to your advantage

The Internet is a wonderful tool and can add significant capability to your abilities both personally and as an organization. Used correctly, the Internet can help to make you

22

and your organization more efficient, faster and more responsive to your customers and staff. Here are some pointers to help you get the most from the technology.

Transferring files

As we just explained, the Internet is a great way to move files from anywhere in the world to anywhere else in the world for the cost of a local call. This means that if you need to send a document, spreadsheet, report or image to someone else and there is very little time to do it you no longer have to panic about when to book the courier for. You can send any of these things across the Net. Not only that, but you can send files such as sound files and images.

Instant messaging

Wouldn't it be great if you could have an interactive exchange of messages with someone thousands of miles away, all for the price of a local call. Well you can – it's called instant messaging. As well as being commonly available for your computer, this software is also available through many of the Internet e-mail sites as instant messaging or 'buddy' messaging. Some systems can even be set up so that you input a list of people with whom you would like to exchange messages and the system will tell you as soon as they log on to the Internet. This is very useful when you want to get a quick answer from, say, someone who is in a different time zone and you don't want to wait until they have trawled through all of their e-mails to find and respond to the e-mail that you sent.

Internet telephony

The advantage of using the Internet to make telephone calls is that you only pay for the local call between your location and your ISP. The ISP then takes care of all of the telephone connections between their 'point of presence' and wherever the person you are calling plugs into the Net. So if you are in Europe and the person you are calling is in the United States or, say, Japan you and the person you are calling each pay for a local call and the ISP pays for the rest. (Good deal!)

With such a great invention you would think that it would need a lot of equipment but that's not the case. All you need is a small piece of software that is easily obtainable (and increasingly comes packaged in the latest versions of the major browsers), a sound card and speakers (most new systems already have these for games, music, etc), and lastly a microphone (these are very cheap). Then the faster your line speed and connector are the better but anything better than 28.8 kbps will suffice.

Videoconferencing

Another vast opportunity to save time and money, especially as the commercial world becomes more global, is videoconferencing. Meetings via video link have really taken off over the last few years and are commonplace in the United States where executives are increasingly reluctant to jump on planes and travel great distances just to spend an hour or so in a meeting that could be perfectly well accomplished via a videoconference. Videoconference facilities can be hired and are usually very expensive but with just a little equipment you can do the same over the Internet. Videoconferencing works in the same way as Internet telephony – you just add a camera. In fact, some telephones that incorporate a camera are now available but you can just as easily buy the two items separately and use them together. Some laptops such as Sony's Vaio include a video camera built in to the top edge of the screen so that you can videoconference on the move.

Telephone and video conferencing also have the advantage that a number of people can be linked in at the same time (easier to do with telephone conferencing than video) and it is possible to use the computer screen at each point of the link to show drawings, documents or text messages at the same time as the conference is in progress.

TIP

Microsoft's NetMeeting software has real-time voice and video conferencing plus collaborative application sharing, collaborative document editing, background file transfer (which means that it goes on in the background and does not disrupt the other things that you are doing whilst this is happening) and a whiteboard that everyone at the 'Net meeting' can see and use to draw on. Even better, it's free with Windows 98 and Internet Explorer. You can also get the latest version by downloading it from the extensive Microsoft Web site at www.microsoft.com/netmeeting.

Sources of information

There are over a billion pages on the Web and more are being added every day. One of the key skills in being able to conduct useful research is therefore that of finding relevant sites with the information you want. To help you do this there are a few tools that really work. These are search engines, directories, newsgroups, mailing lists and bookmarks.

A search engine is a powerful database that tries to keep up with the huge number of sites on the Web and list them all. Search engines have two ways of adding to their lists of sites. They send out roving programs that look for new sites and then read the keywords that are attached to the home page of these sites for the search engine's use.

The second way they have is through site owners sending in details of their sites and asking to be listed. Some search engines try to list everything whilst there are others that specialize in just one or two areas. Remember, once you have found the site you want you can bookmark it.

Directories limit themselves to a relatively few links, perhaps only a hundred thousand and they specialize in well-defined listings for a particular area.

Newsgroups are another part of the Internet outside of the World Wide Web. These can be accessed through specialist newsgroup sites such as UUnet.com or by going to the newsgroup option at your ISP's home page. Newsgroups are meeting places for people who want to swap information and news on a particular subject. You will find just about every subject you can possibly think of is covered and most newsgroup viewers will have a search facility to help you.

Mailing lists are a very specific source of research; they are often described as 'serious' or 'grown up' newsgroups. They are probably one of the best ways of accessing experts in various fields and are definitely worth trying out.

Getting useful statistics and other data

There are a number of very useful government sites that publish a range of reports and surveys. Another great source are the newspapers and periodicals. Many of the specialist publications have a Web presence and on many of these you can search for articles ranging back over the last few years. There are also some specialist services such as the one at FT.com that promises to give you an overview of a number of different industries, including the major issues that those industries are currently facing. You can also use newsgroups and bulletin boards to ask about issues and where the good sites are to find out what you need to know. All in all, the Internet is the world's largest and most comprehensive reference library so, as they say in New York, 'if you can't find it here, it don't exist'.

News services that keep you up to date

There are an increasing number of sites that will keep you up to date on just about any topic from newsletter services that regularly mail you about what's happening in a particular industry, to travel companies that will send details of special offers. There are also those such as share trading services that will send real-time 'alerts' when a stock movement happens that you have programmed a 'trigger' for, or news services that will send a message to your mobile with the same. The latter type of site has seen a huge rise in business and the ability to send text messages to mobile telephones and the advent of WAP is expected to increase that growth even further.

Business-to-business Web sites

Business-to-business, or B2B, Web sites are the fastest growing part of the Web and they offer a wealth of benefits to businesses of all sizes.

In essence, B2B is about giving smaller and medium sized enterprises (often called SMEs by IT suppliers) the same power as their larger brethren. How is this done? Well, there are basically two areas: exchanges and services.

Let's imagine that you want to buy your stationery for the year. A business-to-business exchange can allow you to put out a request for quotations. You specify what you want to buy and the ideal quantity and post it to a bulletin board. The bulletin board is read by thousands of traders of different types, many of which may be printers. Those that are printers can e-mail their quotations for your requirements. If you decide to accept one, you simply e-mail back acceptance. The system works well for both buyer and seller because it cuts the costs for both sides.

In the example above, the item that you want to buy is unique because it is customized to you; however if the item that you want to buy is not unique, let's say a computer, then you can use a B2B exchange as part of a buying group and make savings that way. Some exchanges that run buying groups are either owned or founded by one or a number of companies that are already themselves big buyers but they have realized that if they are joined by a host of smaller companies this further increases their buying power. These sites are especially attractive because of the degree of professionalism and knowledge of the buyers involved, which as a member of the exchange you effectively get for free

Other types of sites provide Web-based business services such as legal services, marketing, accountancy, tax advice, printing and many more. Virgin run one of the UK's better sites of this kind at www.virginbiz.com. These businesses allow organizations to not only find specialized services such as tax advice specializing in vertical markets but they also offer the possibility of contracting out many of the areas of a business that do not contribute to the competitiveness of the organization. For this reason they are becoming ever more popular as the trend towards highly leveraged companies grows.

Formulating a usage policy

One of the concerns of many business people when considering whether or not they should 'connect' their business is a fear that the facility could be misused. However
there are many tools available to help you ensure that you
get the maximum benefits from the Internet and minimize
the potential downside. The answer to ensuring that you
get the best from connecting your business, though, lies
not just with software – you also need to set usage of the
new facilities within an 'acceptable use' policy.

The function of an acceptable use policy is firstly to pro-
tect your organization from harm, both through potential
litigation and potential systems damage through viruses or
other harmful invasion. A good policy, however, can also
have a second function: to help guide users within your
organization to get the best from using the facilities.

Whilst, in many countries, there exists a body of law surrounding the acceptable use of e-mail and the protection of
personal or sensitive data, the laws around the rights of
employees to access the Internet whilst at work are less
well defined and are being moulded over time by case law.

An increasing number of cases are being brought against
employees who have been deemed by their employer to
have used Internet and/or e-mail facilities inappropriately.
In these cases it has generally been found by the courts
that the employer has the right to monitor access and
usage of the facilities they provide and to act if employees'
use is not in accordance with policy or guidance notes that
have been issued.

Those cases that have been brought have usually centred
on the dismissal of an employee for abuse of e-mail or
Internet access where the applicable law in the country concerned has been that regarding indecency, sexual harass-

ment or the law of contract. In such areas it has generally been seen by the courts as entirely reasonable for a company to act against individuals breaking any one of these laws. However, there are other legal implications that you should consider when formulating an acceptable use policy, such as the laws on copyright and the law surrounding the proper use and security of personal or protected data.

Virus protection is also, of course, a huge area that needs careful management. We deal with this in the next chapter of this book and look at software that can re-enforce your usage policy with access controls as well as provide virus protection.

In general the lessons to be learnt from litigation and practice to date are:

- Ensure that the policy that you formulate is clear and unequivocal.

- Ensure that every employee is issued with a copy.

- Ensure that the policy document is regularly kept up to date.

- If you revise your policy, reissue a guidance note to every employee.

- Prevention is better than cure – install specialist software that can reinforce your policy by restricting access to undesirable sites, monitor invasive threats to your systems and monitor e-mail transmissions.

If you do all of this then you should steer clear of potential problems and if you do unfortunately have to become involved in litigation you will, at least, have a good platform from which to make your case.

3

E-MAIL

E-mail is by far the most used application on the Internet. In part, that popularity comes not just because it allows you to send a 'letter' to someone else but also because you can attach photographs, documents and even movies and sound and send them anywhere in the world virtually instantly, for the price of a local call. E-mail is also available on an increasing number of devices such as mobile phones, PDAs, televisions and even e-mail phones for the home.

How e-mail works

In the same way as every Web site on the Internet has a unique name so that traffic can be directed to it, every e-mail address also has to be unique so that messages to that mail address go there and nowhere else. To do this, an e-mail name is made up of two parts: 1) the site name at which the e-mail address is 'resident' (which is, of course, already unique) and 2) the name of the recipient (which must also be a unique name). The two are joined together by the @ sign.

For example, our Web site is StevenArmstrong.com and so an e-mail addressed to me would be addressed as:

StevenArmstrong@StevenArmstrong.com

Getting an e-mail address/types of account

One of the advantages of owning your own Web site is that you can have e-mail addresses to whomever @ your Web site's name. If you do not have your own Web site then you will need to set up an e-mail address at an e-mail services Web site and therefore your e-mail address will be your-name @ the provider's site name.

There are a host of e-mail providers on the Internet such as Hotmail, AOL, Freeserve, CompuServe and Virgin, as well as ones that combine e-mail services with fax and other services such as YAC. Whichever you choose you should be able to sign up online without a great deal of fuss. The drawback with many of these services is that if your name is, say, John or Jane Brown, you are unlikely to get your name @ the provider's address.com – you are more likely to end up with a name such as jbrown123456789 @ the provider's name .com. This is because the system needs to give every subscriber a unique address and if there are many jbrowns who want to have an e-mail address from that provider's service they will need a prefix to identify them all uniquely. This is OK and in fact even though there are millions of names already in use, many people still manage to think of one that is fitting and unique. The problem is that these are rarely good e-mail names to use for business and professional communications. Bassmental@AOL.com, for example, may not be ideal as a business address unless you are either a bass guitarist or someone who sells them. For this reason many organizations have their own Web site through which they can provide e-mail names for all of their employees. For example, my company is called Steven Armstrong consulting and it has its own Web site called StevenArmstrong.com, my e-mail address there is Stevenarmstrong@stevenarmstrong.com, other employees all have an e-mail address there and they can be called by name or by title or even just by department such as Webmaster@stevenarmstrong.com or just booksales@steve-narmstrong.com. In each case we manage the mail as it arrives so that it is dealt with appropriately.

Managing your e-mail

It is important for any organization to manage its e-mail effectively and yet this is not always as simple as it should be. The biggest problem that you are likely to encounter with e-mail is the sheer volume of e-mails that you are likely to receive on a day-to-day basis, which explains why devices capable of collecting e-mail to read whilst away from the office, such as WAP phones and PDAs, are becoming so popular.

There are, however, things that you can do to minimize the stress on yourself and on others:

- Use flags. These are included in almost all mail systems and they allow you to set priorities such as Urgent/Not Urgent/For Information Only, etc. One can also sort e-mail by priority in most systems to prioritize responding.

- Always give a clear indication of the reason for the message in the subject bar. This will help the recipient and often means your message is dealt with more quickly. Ask others to do the same.

- Most e-mail systems have filters, some of which are capable of very complex rules – learn how yours work and use them; they will prove invaluable once you have mastered them.

30 Minutes . . . To Master the Internet

Confidentiality and security

E-mail is often presumed to be a secure method of communication; in fact it's anything but. In reality there are a wide variety of tools available on the Internet that provide software for intercepting e-mail and anyone from outside or even inside your organization could, without a great deal of difficulty, intercept and read your e-mail unless it is protected.

Protection comes in two forms. The first is a way of ensuring that your message is not changed in any way en route; this is called a digital signature. The second is a way of encrypting the message so that it cannot be read by anyone en route.

Digital signatures

Digital signing is something that is becoming increasingly common and something you should use for any e-mail that is of a commercial or sensitive nature. A digital signature ensures that the message that you have sent arrives without having been altered en route. A digital signature not only 'freezes' the message but it also proves who sent it. By using a digital signature for an important message you can be sure that it will arrive as you sent it and the receiver can be sure that they have received it as you sent it and that it was you who sent it to them. Most e-mail systems have an option in the compose/write function to sign the message with a digital signature.

E-mail encryption

Basic encryption is included now in most e-mail systems with an option to use or not use for each message individually.

34

These systems offer a good basic level of security. They do have one major flaw though and that is that they generally work on a mail-by-mail basis, ie you have to set the encryption option for each e-mail in the same way as you set the priority flag or assign a digital signature. If you want a greater level of protection or if you have a large population of e-mail users that you want to ensure always use encrypted messages then buy one of the specialist packages that integrate with whichever mail system you are using. These sit on your computer or on the server that serves the organization's network. You may want to think carefully though before you go down this route, as encryption can be costly.

JARGON BUSTER

You may hear the term PGP used in relation to e-mail encryption. The term means Pretty Good Privacy and is used most commonly to refer to commonly available encryption that comes as standard with many e-mail packages. PGP means just that – it's pretty good but you can get more protection with specialist packages.

Virus protection

One of the very useful tools that e-mail provides is an easy way of sending files to someone else. A file can be, for example, a word-processed document, such as a contract, or it may be a spreadsheet or a photograph or slide presentation; even sounds and music can be sent this way. To send a file to someone else simply attach the file to the e-mail and send. All good office software packages will have a way of attaching a file to an e-mail and all of the top

Internet-based mail services also have good and reliable ways of attaching and sending files.

The downside to this facility is that someone can, either deliberately or inadvertently, send you an e-mail with a virus attached to it. Some particularly nasty viruses have been propagated this way. The 'I love you' virus reeked havoc in 1999 when it was sent out onto the Internet, as once inside someone's system it was able to read his or her address book and send itself to everyone whose e-mail address was listed. The title was deliberately designed to entice the recipient to open it, and once opened the virus attached to the e-mail crashed the system it had entered.

JARGON BUSTER

The virus mentioned above was able to attach to an e-mail by using a commonly used file such as a Word file as a 'carrier'. Carriers act as 'Trojan horses' enabling the virus to remain hidden until the file is opened. This type of virus is therefore often referred to as a 'Trojan'.

There are only a very few types of file that cannot carry a virus, such as image files and simple Web pages. However, beware as many complex Web pages download small programs known as applets onto your machine without you knowing – these files certainly can contain viruses. The only way to be sure that you are and remain virus free is to run an anti-virus system that scans all incoming files and provides a 'shield' around your system. The best ones of these have 'live updates', a utility that can download a shield against all of the latest viruses. You can usually run a live update procedure as many times as you want and whenever you want once you have subscribed to the service. Live updates are an essential utility as there are literally hundreds of new viruses discovered every week and the live update mechanism means that you can easily ensure that you have the latest protection against them on a regular basis.

JARGON BUSTER

Once upon a time it became highly fashionable to name anything to do with the Internet after coffee – yes coffee! Hence there are such things as Java (a programming language), Hot Java (a 'hot' version of Java), Beans (little programs – presumably tasting of coffee) and Cookies (see below).

Whilst we are on the subject of security it is worth mentioning 'cookies'. Cookies are little crumb-sized programs left behind on your machine after you have visited a Web site that uses them. A cookie captures information about what you looked at when you went to the site and details of things like your name if you typed them in anywhere whilst visiting the site and stores them on the hard drive of your machine where it can find them again later. The idea is that when you return to the site in question it uses the cookie to recognize you and can do things like greet you by name or suggest that they now have a new super coffee maker that you might like to buy. These can be very useful, for example you can set up your favourite portal such as, say, MSN or Excite to show you a customized view with the latest news, sports, etc that you are interested in, whenever you enter. It knows who you are and when you

37

last visited and what your customization is via a cookie. Some sites though want to read not only their own cookie but anyone else's cookies that have been left on your machine and programs called (you guessed it) 'Cookie Monsters' can do just that.

TIP

You can make sure that no one leaves a cookie on your system; there is a simple switch in the security settings for most browsers that enables you to turn 'support for cookies' off. The downside to this is that you will lose lots of nice features like being able to customize your favourite portal.

Whilst the cookies or applets left behind by reputable sites will be what they claim to be and should hold no danger, other less reputable sites may use cookies or applets to access your system. For example, the details of credit cards or bank account details stored on the system in programs such as spreadsheets or accounting programs are vulnerable to being read and transmitted to a third party.

E-mails are legal documents!

Whilst e-mails may look like fun, informal documents be warned, you can be held responsible for what is contained within them and the content of them can be legally binding. Part of any policy surrounding use and access to the Internet must also be concerned with putting in place a policy to ensure that you and other employees of your company do not fall foul of the law, inadvertently or otherwise. It is essential that you do not leave your organization potentially exposed.

Reading e-mail offline and saving money

Many of the software packages that you will be using to write and view e-mails will have tools to allow you to compose and read e-mails offline. Unless your business is permanently connected, in which case it makes no difference, you should ask anyone using e-mail to compose and read e-mail offline. There is really no sense in incurring line usage charges when you are reading an e-mail or just typing in a message prior to sending it. Tools such as Microsoft's Outlook Express have wizards that enable you to set up your system to go online briefly to send new mail and to retrieve mail from in boxes at Internet mail sites such as Hotmail. The system simply connects, sends mail you have written and is ready to go (you can keep drafts and half-finished ones in a separate area and these won't be posted) and collects mail from one or as many mailboxes as you have set it up for. The system then hangs up immediately it has finished and so the time you spend online is reduced to the absolute minimum.

By using these tools mail is downloaded onto your computer and you can then access them whenever you wish without going online.

As we referred to earlier, such systems can even be set up so that mail is sorted into folders according to criteria such as recipient's name, sender's name or key words, eg any mail that contains the words 'Steven Armstrong' or have been sent to Steven Armstrong can be sorted into a folder called Steven Armstrong. Those for 'webmaster' can be sorted into a folder for the webmaster and so on.

JARGON BUSTER

A 'wizard' is a help program that will guide you through a process. (Such as setting up a connection to retrieve mail from your e-mail account and download it to your PC).

Fax gateways and e-mail to mobiles

There are an increasing number of services aimed at bringing all of the many possible ways that a customer or colleague can contact you together into one place. Message facilities on mobile telephones, landline telephones, e-mail, faxes and SMS message services are all converging and it's becoming increasingly common to have messages from all of these services directed to either your e-mail account or your mobile telephone.

You can therefore have e-mail messages directed to your mobile telephone as a text message, or your voice messages to your mobile directed to your e-mail as sound files attached to e-mails. You can also have faxes treated the same way with faxes converted to e-mails and vice versa. All of these services offer the ability for you to be 'always in contact'. These 'gateways' are commonly found at the home page of your e-mail service or Internet service providers but there are also specialist companies worth looking at such as www.YAC.com (You're Always Connected) who offer a comprehensive service at minimal cost.

E-mail as a marketing tool

E-mail can be a very powerful marketing tool, as many businesses have already discovered. E-mail can be used to send out one-off e-mail messages in much the same way as direct mail is used in the conventional mail sense or it can be used in a more timely and interactive way.

One of the best uses of e-mail as a marketing tool is to link it to a database facility on your Web site through the inclusion of a form, which the visitor fills out whilst at your site. This form then updates a database with the details that the visitor has just typed in. In this way you can invite visitors to your site to register for regular news, special offers, product updates, etc, all delivered by e-mail. Some sites even demand that you register by making registration a prerequisite to being allowed to view the rest of the site after you have visited the home page. There are, of course, implications regarding the protection of data obtained and held in this way and we look at this further in Chapter 5.

Databases are generally easy to set up on a site but the maintenance can be a little more tricky and in general the larger the number of addresses that you want to keep, the more you move towards needing specialist help. There are companies that will administer your database for you and even mail out the e-mails to people on your database. There are also specialist companies such as Oracle, the world's biggest database provider, who can offer lots of help and advice.

Another method is to buy in a list of e-mail addresses from a list broker. This is particularly useful if you want to reach a large number of people but don't have either a large enough 'go to' site to attract the number of people you want or if you haven't been running long enough to gather as many names as you require. If you want to use a list broker, though, make sure that you use an 'opt-in' broker who is a member of a professional direct mail association.

JARGON BUSTER

An 'opt-in' list is one where e-mail addresses are collected from people who elect (opt-in) to give their details explicitly. This type of list is generally of higher quality than those where people have not explicitly given their permission to be mailed. You also know that the recipient is willing to receive e-mails advertising products and services. This is also generally better for you than one who is not.

4

BUILDING A WEB SITE

Building your own Web site can be remarkably easy and doesn't need to absorb huge amounts of money. However, one thing that a Web site does absorb, that is arguably more valuable than money, is time. Almost 40 per cent of Web sites are abandoned in their first year according to surveys conducted by the major ISPs and one of the primary reasons for this is the commitment required by the author to maintain and make its content attractive to viewers.

Which type of Web site do you want?

Before embarking upon owning a Web site you should consider carefully what it is that you want the site to achieve and whether a Web site is the most cost-effective way of achieving it. In this chapter we will help you work through many of the considerations. The first being that, in effect, there are only two types of Web site: 1) those that are there purely for information and 2) those that are there to sell something.

One of the things that the Web is very good at doing, in fact the thing that it is probably the best at doing, is in providing a place where information can be viewed by many people. This, in fact, should be no surprise as the Web's original purpose was to be used as a tool to make information available to a large population of academics and researchers who wanted to disseminate their knowledge. Its great attraction is that you need only say something once. If a million people then want to know what you have said they can all look it up rather than ask you individually. It's no wonder then that businesses who needed, or wanted, to tell a lot of people the same thing, saw a way of doing so at a fraction of the cost of other channels of communication.

How to build your site

Building your own site is actually not as difficult as you may think. A Web site is simply a collection of HTML pages that are linked together. If you are used to putting together presentations in a slide presentation package such as Microsoft PowerPoint you will have little difficulty in getting to grips with the idea of putting together a number of pages as a Web site. There are, however, three deadly mistakes that it is all too easy to make when you put your Web site together for the first time. Firstly, unlike a presentation that you are giving in person, the viewer of a Web site can choose the order in which they view your pages. This means that you need to plan the site so that whichever 'path' your visitors take around your site it still makes sense. Secondly, and perhaps even more difficult to master, is the issue of 'content'. A Web site must have very good content otherwise people will simply go elsewhere, or look once but not come back. Lastly, you do need to ensure that your site works – broken links (ones that don't work) and graphics that don't work or pages that take too long to load or are too crowded with flashing, spinning graphics are all too easy to invent.

JARGON BUSTER

Web site designers may talk about how 'sticky' a site is. By this they mean: Is the site designed in such a way that once having found it visitors will want to stay for a while and not leave to try something else?

Using Web-building tools

One of the best ways to build a Web site is to use a specialist tool such as FrontPage (from Microsoft), Fusion (from NetObjects) or Dreamweaver (from Adobe). These tools allow you to build Web pages without having to know HTML, the programming language for building Web pages. With many of these tools you simply 'drag and drop' and 'cut and paste', in the same way as you do with word-processing and slide presentation packages. Another advantage is that you install these software packages on your computer and develop the whole site offline. The packages usually give you the facility to see how the pages that you are developing will look online and some, such as Microsoft FrontPage, will even tell you how long a page that you have developed will take to load at various line speeds. You can then experiment with 'tuning' the page by reducing the size of graphics, etc, until you are happy. Once you are satisfied with the result you then upload the Web site to a Web hosting service such as Microsoft's.

Using template Web sites

If you are not used to making good presentations or are worried about your ability to incorporate a sense of style into your site then you should consider using a template provided by a Web hosting service. Many of the hosting services provide templates and they are usually highly customizable. A template service will provide you with a choice of different page types; for example, they may offer: pages with one, two or three spaces for graphics; album pages where you can have a number of photographs in thumbnail size; links pages, and so on. Very often these sites also offer other facilities such as guest books, survey forms, links to e-mail and more. You simply select the type of page that you want to use, give it a title and then add the text and graphics that you want to show on that page, click 'OK' and it's done. Other things such as menus, page titles, layout, etc are all handled by the template design. Most of these schemes offer a selection of templates geared to different industries and uses. The templates themselves are also usually quite customizable, allowing you to choose backgrounds, colours and layout styles as well as inserting your own logo. While you can do all of these things with the Web building tools, the advantage of the template approach is that you don't have to learn any Web site design skills and you can concentrate on getting the look and the content right rather than the programming. If you then decide to pick up some HTML skills later you can usually come back to your template and incorporate HTML commands to make your site even better while still retaining the benefits of the template.

> ### TIP
>
> Template sites also have another set of benefits – they are usually supported by a number of optional extras such as services to automatically submit your site details to search engines and to upgrade simple information-only sites to full blown commercial sites with shopping carts and credit card processing later if you wish.

Of course, template sites charge more for using various services than sites that simply host an uploaded site that is already complete but because the market is so competitive the difference between paying more per month rather than laying out on the initial cost of site-building software may be less than would first appear if you make that calculation.

> ### TIP
>
> Some hosting companies have 'try before you buy' schemes that allow you to build a site using their templates and try it for a short period (up to a month usually) before confirming that you want to keep it. This allows you to look at the templates available and to try your hand at designing a site without the outlay of expensive software or services.

Using a Web site designer

Of course, the ultimate is to use a Web site design service and have everything done for you and there are some very good designers around. Of course, you need to be careful when choosing your designer, as you would be when choosing any form of builder in any other walk of life. Ask for references and take your time during the initial discussions to satisfy yourself that the designer understands your objectives for your site. Be clear at the outset about the charging structure and the expectation around payment as well as those success criteria which will determine payment.

Acquiring a domain name

One of the key things that will either help or hinder your success on the Web is the domain name that you choose for your site. The name that follows the 'www' part of the address is called your domain name and it consists of three elements:

- A name.
- An organization code, such as '.co' (for commercial companies), '.org' (for non profit-making organizations and '.gov' (for government and governmental bodies).
- A country code, such as '.uk' (for the United Kingdom), '.fr' (for France) and so on.

The exception to this rule is the United States and that is because in its early years the Web was primarily used by US companies and the organization that allocates domains is in the United States, and so the United States is the only country that does not need a country code as the Web assumes that everyone is in the United States unless told otherwise! For this reason, US companies only need use '.com' with no country code after it and this is why 'dot-com' has become synonymous with having a Web presence. However, you don't have to be in the United States to have dotcom after your name. Our Web site, for example, is www.StevenArmstrong.com but we are not based in the United States. How can this be? Well, the country code system has really fallen into disrepair. The global nature of cyberspace doesn't really care where you are physically, it just wants you to have a unique address so that it can find you out of all of the millions of addresses on the system. If you look back at Chapter 2 you will see how it works and the fact that every address on the Internet is registered with one of the registrar companies. In practice your ISP will usually register your name for you and so long as it is unique you can use '.com' or '.co.uk' or dot whatever. There are companies that specialize in domain names and they are readily accessible on the Net; many have search engines that allow you to see if your name is already in use. You can buy your name directly from these domain name brokers and the costs are usually very competitive. After buying your name you will receive, in the post, a certificate showing your ownership of the name.

The things that they don't normally tell you

One of the things that they don't normally tell you (or at least they do but it's hard to spot) is that you need to renew your domain name registration on a regular basis, usually annually, or you lose it.

Another thing that they don't tell you is that in the same way that there are domain name brokers there are also companies that specialize in looking at the dates that names are due for renewal and if you fail to renew they pounce on the good ones and register them to themselves.

TIP

There are some very interesting country codes such as '.fm', '.cv' and '.tv', the latter belonging to Tuvalu, a small island in the South Pacific of 9,000 people (at the last count). With a little imagination it is possible to make up a very interesting and memorable name by using the combination of name and organization and country code, for example the combination '.co.ma' actually exists.

Adding animation to your site

One of the things that sets apart the professional Web site from the amateur one is the inclusion of good graphic content, especially animated graphics. Animation in particular can transform an otherwise dull page into a lively and attractive one that will make people want to read it. It can be very easy, though, to overdo it and end up with a page where too many graphics start to work against one another and become too distracting for the viewer.

It is actually a lot easier to include animated graphics on your Web site than you think. There are many sites on the Web that give away free graphics and animations: these are called 'clip art' sites. You will find many clip art sites through your search engine. Once at one of these sites there are usually a huge number of graphics available free of charge, indexed by category. Find through the index the graphic or animation that you want and simply right click on your mouse. Choose the 'save as' option and save it to a directory on your computer where you can easily find it again with a name that will help you remember what it is.

When you then either paste this image into your Web page (if you are using a Web building tool) or upload it to your Web site (if you are using a template) it should appear on your page exactly as it appeared on the clip art Web site's page.

Internal Web sites

As we said at the beginning of this chapter, one of the things that a Web site does extremely well is it lets you tell a lot of people something in a very efficient way and without a great deal of work or overhead. It is worth considering then utilizing this to improve communication **inside** your organization. A Web site does not have to be hosted on the Internet – it can be hosted on a server on your internal network and therefore only accessible by the people within your organization. What a wonderful tool then to get a message across to the workforce or to provide information that will help people be more efficient and able to service your customers and each other better.

The unique mix of text, graphics and hyperlinks means that you have the world's most wonderful communications tools at your disposal and the key to efficiency is communication, communication, communication. An internal Internet or 'Intranet' can hold information on any subject and you can let the organization's employees contribute. In this way, information that is currently locked up in files, documents or people's heads can be turned into knowledge that all can share.

5

BUILDING A WEB BUSINESS

Building a Web business is more than just building your Web site. The World Wide Web is a very large place and to balance the sheer size of the opportunity open to you are the number of other Web sites competing for attention in competition to your own. In this chapter we look at some of the considerations that you should understand and plan for.

Is it true what they say about millions of people coming to my Web site?

Possibly!

The size of the potential marketplace is stupendously large; however, in counterbalance the number of sites vying for attention is also proportionately large. Unless you have something that everyone in the world wants to beat a path to your door for then you will have to work hard to get people to find your site amongst the vast number of other sites out there.

In simplistic mode, there are only two things you need to do: 1) get people to visit your site; and 2) get people to come back for second and subsequent visits. This is quite apart from selling them something whilst they are there. If this sounds terribly easy then you may be in for a shock. However, if you can master these two aspects, then you may be in for a fortune, or at least a pay rise!

What sells on the Internet?

Well, some things sell well and others not at all. Some of the 'Internet watchers', the consultancy companies who regularly conduct market research, can provide some very accurate and interesting data. As suggested in a previous chapter, you can find such research easily on the Net itself. However, there are some generalities that seem to hold true which are worth thinking about when planning your Web business.

The Internet is an 'immediate' medium. In general, people shopping on the Internet want delivery of their purchase quickly and easily. This has proved a problem with items that are 'bigger than a letterbox' as it means that these items cannot be posted through the front door and this means that either delivery needs to be made when and where people are available to take it, or you need a place where people can go to make a collection.

Another generality is that many people remain sceptical about using their credit cards to purchase goods from sites where they have little or no reassurance about safety, either through a well-known brand name or through appropriate messages at the site itself.

Taking money

If you want to run a commercial Web site then you must be able to accept credit cards and process them in a secure manner. What is more, you should take every opportunity in your site's design to inform your potential customers of the level of protection that you have provided to make their transactions secure.

Shopping carts

The first thing that you will need on the site is a shopping cart. Shopping cart software allows your customer to add things to the cart (sometimes called a basket) that they wish to purchase as they browse the site and before they proceed to a checkout where they pay for those items. The shopping cart software can be bought from specialist suppliers, again findable through the Web. Alternatively, if your site hosting service has a 'shop' option, it will include this software automatically for you. A full service shop option will also help you accept credit card transactions, which is vital if you want to succeed in selling via the Internet.

Credit card transactions

In order to actually take the money, though, you will need two things.

First, to authorize the card in real time. To do this you will have to set up a special authorizing account with a card processing company. Every country has a number of card processors and their rules differ; however one thing that you can be sure of is that they all take a percentage (usually around 4 per cent) of every transaction.

Second, in order to be able to link to and work with the card processor you will also need an Internet credit card merchant account. If you bank with a major clearing bank they should be able to help you with this for all major credit cards except AmEx (who do everything differently!). The company that provides these facilities will also take a percentage of every transaction and this is also generally around 4 per cent.

If you already take credit cards you will still have to go through the system above to process payments over the Net.

TIP

Making the links work between your system and the card processor's system can be difficult and there is no real incentive for them to fix a problem, if one occurs. This often means that you will end up paying someone to come in and fix the problem. This commonly being the case you may want to hire someone at the outset to ensure that the links are working and robust. It may prove cheaper than doing it later.

The costs then are worth keeping a careful eye on. With authorization charges and processing charges and costs associated with the hosting of the Web site itself and specialist software such as carts, as well as the possibility of paying for expert services, you may find that your profit margin is seriously eroded. If on top of this there are costs in the supply chain or for delivery or distribution then you may want to revisit your business plan. Certainly, any financiers to whom you put a business plan will already have very good experience and know very precisely these costs, so you will have to have good figures before you approach them. Altogether, it's not surprising that some people wonder who is really taking the money from whom in the shopping malls of cyberspace.

Digital money and electronic wallets

There are many technological alternatives to credit cards and notes and coins in the hyperspace shopping mall of the future. Digital money is one that you are likely to hear mentioned. This form of electronic money is still not widely accepted but will be worth watching in the future. Go to www.digicash.com to read more on digital money from one of the pioneers in the field. Also worth keeping an eye on are electronic wallets, which are being pushed hard by people such as Microsoft; the Microsoft Web site is a good place to start for information on this. Also likely to be one of the emerging technologies in the coming few years is the payment standard SET.

SET

You may also come across people talking about SET, the Secure Electronic Transaction Standard pioneered, amongst others, by VISA who are better known for their credit card organization. Although SET has many advantages in terms of the security facilities it offers, it has not yet been widely adopted, despite its parentage. You can find out more about the technology and recent developments as well as how well the take-up of the standard is going at the SET homepage at www.setco.org and there is also information at the VISA site at www.visa.com.

Data protection

Following on from considering the implications of taking payment over the Internet and completing our look at potential legal implications of Internet technologies is the subject of data protection. This is an area that certainly carries the full force of the law. Almost every country has well-defined data protection legislation, usually enforced by statutory rights of disclosure, a 'watchdog' body and draconian penalties for transgressors.

In essence, if you procure information either through a payment transaction or by a visitor to your sight volunteering information, for example by filling in a database form, you must be very careful with that data and hold it securely. As part of formulating an Internet usage policy you should have clear rules associated with passing on information to third parties. Check what you are allowed to do under the specific national laws of the country(s) in which you operate before you pass on details, or comments about details, on data you hold to another party. In practice it is wise not to hold any data that you do not require directly for business or marketing purposes. If you intend to pass on data to another party, either as a commercial venture or as a co-marketing venture, be explicit at the point where the data is collected. Tell the person who is about to give you data that it may be passed on and under what circumstances it may be passed on. Give the person concerned the choice of opting in or opting out. This will stand you in good stead should you then be challenged by litigation.

Lastly, be aware that Data Protection legislation covers the storage of information and this can include archived as well as current data. It also often gives rights of access to view information held.

Getting listed on search engines

Most people who visit a site find it through a search engine. Of all of the sites that come up in a search, the majority of people only look at the first page – that's three to seven sites, depending upon how the engine displays sites selected. Of all the sites that they visit, the average person will only bookmark a total of seven sites. From these statistics it's easy to see that it's important to not only get listed on the major search engines but also to get as high up the list on the return of a query as you possibly can. To do this you need to add 'meta tags' to the home page of your Web site. Meta tags are words that describe your site to the searching engine. These words need to be the sorts of words that people will pick when asking the search engine a question, eg if someone wants to find a site specializing in travel to Australia, the search engine would look for key words such as Australia, travel, flights, holidays, business travel, etc. You can usually submit up to 30 words to describe your site on a search engine submission.

Submitting to search engines is a very laborious process and each engine will have a different format and take a different amount of time to come back to you and say 'yes' or 'no'. Some of the popular engines, because they have so many submissions, can take six weeks or longer to respond to an application. In addition, there are over 500 main ones and many other specialist ones. Lastly, as if all of that was not enough, if you want to stay current you need to submit to many engines every three weeks or they will assume that you have ceased to exist.

There are services that will take on the task of submitting your site to the top search engines and they are generally well worth the money. Normally the company hosting your site will have a service that you can subscribe to for a monthly fee. If you prefer to do it yourself, there are a number of software packages that automate the process and do what your service provider would do, and some of these are downloadable from the Web.

Every search engine will have a section on its Web site to advise you how to make submissions; whichever route you choose these are still worth reading and taking note of.

Advertising and other ways of promoting your site

Advertising your site is a key requirement if you want to get to the big time. To make your campaign effective you should plan using the various traditional (old) media in conjunction with your Web site's facilities as a planned campaign. For example, you may wish to take an advertisement in the press linked to an editorial on a promotional offer tied to the Web site. Whatever you do, make sure that you can measure the increase in traffic to your site. There are easy ways for you to do this, such as having a counter on the home page so that you can record the number of 'hits' your site gets each day. There are also other more sophisticated tools that can tell you where a visitor to your site came from and where they went afterwards as well as cookies that can tell you what your visitor looked at and so on. Our sister book, *Advertising on the Internet*, gives plenty of advice on planning an effective campaign strategy. Our Web site also has a number of links to tracking and counting software.

Other ways to promote your site are to use banner exchange schemes where a small advertisement for your site is swapped with that of another site in the same banner exchange scheme. You then post their banner on your site and they do the same on their site. This is the most common form of advertising on the Net and is very effective. Many schemes are free apart from an optional set-up fee for the scheme to produce a banner for you.

Some dos and don'ts about Web sites

The best advice about the design of any site is to keep it simple. Make sure that what's on the page is easy to use (not everyone is as intelligent or as computer literate as

59

you). And make sure that it works – I have seen many sites where the facilities are potentially great but just end up being too difficult to use and so I have given up. The latest research suggests that at least 65 per cent of people shopping on the Internet abandon the site in mid purchase.

Give your visitors the chance to communicate with you and have an e-mail link to your webmaster so that faults can be reported.

But above all, ignore the don'ts and do get involved – the Web is a greatly rewarding and forgiving medium and you won't regret the time you spend, whether you are doing it as a service or as a means to earn money.

6

GETTING MORE INFORMATION

As we said at the beginning of this book, the intention of the book is to deliver condensed, high-quality information in 5-minute sections as one would in an executive briefing. Unlike a live, one-to-one, executive briefing, however, a book does not allow an interactive dialogue. In an executive briefing, you can do three things that a book on its own is unable to do:

- you can check your understanding of what you have learnt;

- you can home in on a subject and ask for further information to get a more in-depth understanding of that subject area;

- you can ask questions and get answers from the person giving the briefing.

Our Web site is here to help. At www.stevenarmstrong.com we have put together a comprehensive set of links that relate to topics and technologies mentioned in this book. So if you want to know more about something that we have mentioned generically you can link to the Web sites of those companies providing the technologies or the services to which we have referred and learn more. We also welcome any feedback that you have about any of our books or about the Web site and will be interested to hear if the book has helped you to Master the Internet, which we hope it has.